THE COMPLETE BOOK OF
AIR FRYING

QUICK & EASY RECIPES YOU'LL CRAVE

Publications International, Ltd.

Some of the products listed in this publication may be in limited distribution.

Pictured on the front cover: Curly Air-Fried Fries (*page 122*).

Pictured on the back cover (*top to bottom*): Homemade Air-Fried Bagels (*page 60*) and Mini Pepper Nachos (*page 7*).

Photographs on page 27 © Shutterstock.com.

ISBN: 978-1-64558-114-7

Manufactured in China.

8 7 6 5 4 3 2 1

Microwave Cooking: Microwave ovens vary in wattage. Use the cooking times as guidelines and check for doneness before adding more time.

Let's get social!

 @Publications_International

@PublicationsInternational

www.pilcookbooks.com

TABLE OF
CONTENTS

ENJOY YOUR
AIR FRYER

Do you love fried foods but try to avoid them? You no longer need to worry.

The air fryer is your answer to preparing fried foods without the extra calories, fat, or mess in the kitchen. You'll get the taste, and texture of fried foods—crispy, tasty, and crunchy—that you love and crave, without the added guilt often felt when consuming them. Plus, you'll soon see how your air fryer is so easy to use, cooks food faster, and provides a no-fuss clean up.

You'll love the ability to prepare fried foods in your air fryer, but you'll also soon find that you can prepare all types of other foods, too. Make everything from appetizers to meals to sides and even desserts! Why not try air-fried fruits and pound cake? What about trying marinated salmon or pizza bagels? You'll even love the taste of roasted vegetables. You can bake in it, grill in it, steam in it, roast in it, and reheat in it.

Choose from more than 90 ideas here, or create your own.

Now get started and have fun eating and serving all those healthier foods without the added guilt.

HELPFUL TIPS:

- Read your air fryer's manufacturer's directions carefully before cooking to make sure you understand the specific features of your air fryer before starting to cook.

- Preheat your air fryer for 2 to 3 minutes before cooking.

- You can cook foods typically prepared in the oven in your air fryer. But because the air fryer is more condensed than a regular oven, it is recommended that recipes cut 25°F to 50°F off temperature and 20% off the typical cooking times.

- Avoid having foods stick to your air fryer basket by using nonstick cooking spray or cooking on parchment paper or foil. (Be sure to place food on parchment paper or foil to avoid having it blow around.) You can also get food to brown and crisp more easily by spraying occasionally with nonstick cooking spray during the cooking process.

- Don't overfill your basket. Each air fryer differs in its basket size. Cook foods in batches as needed.

- Use toothpicks to hold food in place. You may notice that light foods may blow around from the pressure of the fan. Just be sure to secure foods in the basket to prevent this.

ENJOY YOUR AIR FRYER

....

- Check foods while cooking by opening the air fryer basket. This will not disturb cooking times. Once you return the basket, the cooking resumes.

- Experiment with cooking times of various foods. Test foods for doneness before consuming—check meats and poultry with a meat thermometer, and use a toothpick to test muffins and cupcakes.

- Use your air fryer to cook frozen foods, too! Frozen French fries, fish sticks, chicken nuggets, individual pizzas—these all work great. Just remember to reduce cooking temperatures and times.

ESTIMATED COOKING TEMPERATURES/TIMES*

FOOD	TEMPERATURE	TIMING
Vegetables (asparagus, broccoli, corn-on-the-cob, green beans, mushrooms, cherry tomatoes)	390°F	5 to 6 min.
Vegetables (bell peppers, cauliflower, eggplant, onions, potatoes, zucchini)	390°F	8 to 12 min.
Chicken (bone-in)	370°F	20 to 25 min.
Chicken (boneless)	370°F	12 to 15 min.
Beef (ground beef)	370°F	15 to 17 min.
Beef (steaks, roasts)	390°F	10 to 15 min.
Pork	370°F	12 to 15 min.
Fish	390°F	10 to 12 min.
Frozen Foods	390°F	10 to 15 min.

This is just a guide. All food varies in size, weight, and texture. Be sure to test your food for preferred doneness before consuming it. Also, some foods will need to be shaken or flipped to help distribute ingredients for proper cooking.

Make note of the temperatures and times that work best for you for continued success of your air fryer.

Enjoy and have fun!

PARTY STARTERS

MINI PEPPER NACHOS

MAKES ABOUT 5 SERVINGS

1 cup frozen corn, thawed

1 can (about 15 ounces) black beans, rinsed and drained

½ cup chopped tomatoes

½ teaspoon salt

20 mini sweet peppers, assorted colors, cut in half lengthwise and seeded

½ cup (2 ounces) shredded Mexican-style taco shredded cheese

½ cup sour cream

1 small avocado, chopped (optional)

2 tablespoons chopped green onion or cilantro (optional)

1. Combine corn, beans, tomatoes and salt in medium bowl. Fill peppers with about 1 tablespoon mixture. Sprinkle with cheese.

2. Preheat air fryer to 370°F. Line basket with foil. Cook peppers 5 to 7 minutes or until cheese is lightly browned and melted. Remove to serving plate.

3. Top with sour cream, avocado and green onion, if desired.

GARLIC ROASTED OLIVES AND TOMATOES

1 cup assorted olives, pitted

1 cup grape tomatoes, halved

4 cloves garlic, sliced

1 tablespoon olive oil

1 tablespoon herbes de Provence

Toasted bread slices

1. Pat olives dry with paper towels.

2. Combine olives, tomatoes, garlic and oil in small bowl. Toss with herbes de Provence; mix well.

3. Preheat air fryer to 370°F. Cook 5 to 7 minutes until browned and blistered, shaking occasionally during cooking. Remove to bowl.

4. Serve with bread.

SERVING SUGGESTION: Try tossing with hot cooked pasta for a main dish.

MINI EGG ROLLS

½ pound ground pork

3 cloves garlic, minced

1 teaspoon minced fresh ginger

¼ teaspoon red pepper flakes

6 cups (12 ounces) shredded coleslaw mix

¼ cup reduced-sodium soy sauce

1 tablespoon cornstarch

1 tablespoon seasoned rice vinegar

½ cup chopped green onions

28 wonton wrappers

Prepared sweet and sour sauce

Chinese hot mustard

1. Combine pork, garlic, ginger and red pepper flakes in large nonstick skillet; cook and stir over medium heat about 4 minutes or until pork is cooked through, stirring to break up meat. Add coleslaw mix; cover and cook 2 minutes. Uncover and cook 2 minutes or until coleslaw mix just begins to wilt.

2. Whisk soy sauce and cornstarch in small bowl until smooth and well blended; stir into pork mixture. Add vinegar; cook 2 to 3 minutes or until sauce is thickened. Remove from heat; stir in green onions.

3. Working with 1 wonton wrapper at a time, place wrapper on clean work surface. Spoon 1 level tablespoon pork mixture across and just below center of wrapper. Fold bottom point of wrapper up over filling; fold side points over filling, forming envelope shape. Moisten inside edges of top point with water and roll egg roll toward top point, pressing firmly to seal. Repeat with remaining wrappers and filling. Spray egg rolls with nonstick cooking spray.

4. Preheat air fryer to 370°F. Cook in batches 3 to 5 minutes or until golden brown. Remove to cooling rack; cool slightly before serving. Serve with sweet and sour sauce and mustard for dipping.

MOZZARELLA STICKS

¼ cup all-purpose flour

2 eggs

1 tablespoon water

1 cup plain dry bread crumbs

2 teaspoons Italian seasoning

½ teaspoon salt

½ teaspoon garlic powder

1 package (12 ounces) string cheese (12 sticks)

1 cup marinara or pizza sauce, heated

1. Place flour in shallow dish. Whisk eggs and water in another shallow dish. Combine bread crumbs, Italian seasoning, salt and garlic powder in third shallow dish.

2. Coat each piece of cheese with flour. Dip in egg mixture, letting excess drip back into bowl. Roll in bread crumb mixture to coat. Dip again in egg mixture and roll again in bread crumb mixture. Refrigerate until ready to cook.

3. Preheat air fryer to 370°F. Line basket with parchment paper; spray with nonstick cooking spray.

4. Cook in batches 8 to 10 minutes, shaking halfway through cooking, until golden brown. Serve with marinara sauce.

PORKY PINWHEELS

MAKES 24 PINWHEELS

1 sheet frozen puff pastry (half of a 17¼-ounce package), thawed

1 egg white, beaten

8 slices bacon, crisp-cooked and crumbled

2 tablespoons packed brown sugar

¼ teaspoon ground red pepper

1. Place pastry on sheet of parchment paper. Brush with egg white.

2. Combine bacon, brown sugar and ground red pepper in small bowl. Sprinkle evenly over top of pastry; press lightly to adhere. Roll pastry jelly-roll style from long end. Wrap in parchment paper. Refrigerate 30 minutes.

3. Preheat air fryer to 370°F. Line basket with parchment paper. Slice pastry into ½-inch-thick slices.

4. Cook in batches 8 to 10 minutes or until light golden brown. Remove to wire racks; cool completely.

CHEESY STUFFED MUSHROOMS

4 ounces Brie cheese, rind removed and cut into ½-inch cubes

8 ounces baby bella mushrooms, stems removed

½ cup seasoned dry bread crumbs

1 tablespoon fresh parsley leaves

2 tablespoons olive oil, divided

1. Insert cube of cheese inside each mushroom cap. Stir bread crumbs, parsley and 1 tablespoon oil in small dish. Top each mushroom with bread crumb mixture. Brush with remaining 1 tablespoon oil.

2. Preheat air fryer to 390°F.

3. Cook in batches 4 to 6 minutes or until topping is lightly browned.

TIP: Recipe can easily be doubled for a larger crowd.

MINI CHICKPEA CAKES

1 can (about 15 ounces) chickpeas, rinsed and drained

1 cup grated carrots

⅓ cup seasoned dry bread crumbs

¼ cup creamy Italian salad dressing, plus additional for dipping

1 egg

1. Coarsely mash chickpeas in medium bowl with fork or potato masher. Stir in carrots, bread crumbs, ¼ cup salad dressing and egg; mix well.

2. Shape chickpea mixture into 24 patties, using about 1 tablespoon mixture for each.

3. Preheat air fryer to 370°F. Spray basket with nonstick cooking spray.

4. Cook in batches 10 minutes, turning halfway through cooking, until lightly browned. Serve warm with additional salad dressing for dipping, if desired.

JALAPEÑO POPPERS

MAKES 20 TO 24 POPPERS

10 to 12 fresh jalapeño peppers*

1 package (8 ounces) cream cheese, softened

1½ cups (6 ounces) shredded Cheddar cheese, divided

2 green onions, finely chopped

½ teaspoon onion powder

¼ teaspoon salt

⅛ teaspoon garlic powder

6 slices bacon, crisp-cooked and finely chopped

2 tablespoons panko bread crumbs

2 tablespoons grated Parmesan or Romano cheese

For large jalapeño peppers, use 10. For small peppers, use 12.

1. Cut each jalapeño pepper** in half lengthwise; remove ribs and seeds.

2. Combine cream cheese, 1 cup Cheddar cheese, green onions, onion powder, salt and garlic powder in medium bowl. Stir in bacon. Fill each pepper half with about 1 tablespoon cheese mixture. Sprinkle with remaining ½ cup Cheddar cheese, panko and Parmesan cheese.

3. Preheat air fryer to 370°F. Line basket with parchment paper or foil.

4. Cook 5 to 7 minutes or until cheese is melted and browned but peppers are still firm.

**Jalapeño peppers can sting and irritate the skin, so wear rubber gloves when handling peppers and do not touch your eyes.

GARLIC BITES

½ of 16-ounce package frozen phyllo dough, thawed to room temperature

¾ cup (1½ sticks) butter, melted

3 large heads garlic, separated into cloves, peeled

½ cup finely chopped walnuts

1 cup Italian-style bread crumbs

1. Remove phyllo from package; unroll and place on large sheet of waxed paper. Cut phyllo crosswise into 2-inch-wide strips. Cover phyllo with large sheet of plastic wrap and damp, clean kitchen towel. (Phyllo dries out quickly if not covered.)

2. Lay 1 strip of phyllo at a time on flat surface; brush immediately with butter. Place 1 clove of garlic at end. Sprinkle 1 teaspoon walnuts along length of strip.

3. Roll up garlic clove and walnuts in strip, tucking in side edges as you roll. Brush with butter; roll in bread crumbs. Repeat with remaining phyllo, garlic, walnuts, butter and bread crumbs.

4. Preheat air fryer to 350°F. Line basket with parchment paper. Cook in batches 6 to 8 minutes or until golden brown. Cool slightly.

TOASTED RAVIOLI

- 1 cup all-purpose flour
- 2 eggs
- ¼ cup water
- 1 cup plain dry bread crumbs
- 1 teaspoon Italian seasoning
- ¾ teaspoon garlic powder
- ¼ teaspoon salt
- ½ cup grated Parmesan cheese
- 2 tablespoons finely chopped fresh parsley (optional)
- 1 package (10 ounces) meat or cheese ravioli, thawed if frozen
- Pasta sauce, heated

1. Place flour in shallow dish. Whisk eggs and water in another shallow dish. Combine bread crumbs, Italian seasoning, garlic powder and salt in third shallow dish. Combine Parmesan cheese and parsley, if desired, in large bowl.

2. Preheat air fryer to 390°F. Poke holes in ravioli with toothpick.

3. Coat ravioli with flour. Dip in egg mixture, letting excess drip back into bowl. Roll in bread crumb mixture to coat. Spray with nonstick cooking spray.

4. Cook in batches 5 to 6 minutes, turning once, until golden brown. Add to bowl with cheese; toss to coat. Serve warm with sauce.

THE BIG ONION

DIPPING SAUCE

- ½ cup light mayonnaise
- 2 tablespoons horseradish
- 1 tablespoon ketchup
- ¼ teaspoon paprika
- ⅛ teaspoon salt
- ⅛ teaspoon ground red pepper
- ⅛ teaspoon dried oregano

ONION

- 1 large sweet onion (about 1 pound)
- ½ cup all-purpose flour
- 1 tablespoon buttermilk
- 2 eggs
- ½ cup panko bread crumbs
- 1 tablespoon paprika
- 1½ teaspoons seafood seasoning

1. For sauce, combine mayonnaise, horseradish, ketchup, ¼ teaspoon paprika, salt, ground red pepper and oregano in small bowl; mix well. Cover and refrigerate until ready to serve.

2. For onion, cut about ½ inch off top of onion and peel off papery skin. Place onion cut side down on cutting board. Starting ½ inch from root, use large sharp knife to make one slice down to cutting board. Repeat slicing all the way around onion to make 12 to 16 evenly spaced cuts. Turn onion over; gently separate outer pieces.

3. Meanwhile, put flour in large bowl. Whisk buttermilk and eggs in another large bowl. Combine panko, 1 tablespoon paprika and seafood seasoning in another bowl.

4. Coat onion with flour, shaking off any excess. Dip entire onion in egg mixture, letting excess drip back into bowl. Then coat evenly with panko.

5. Preheat air fryer to 390°F. Spray basket with nonstick cooking spray.

6. Cook 10 to 12 minutes or until golden brown and crispy. Serve immediately with dipping sauce.

EVERYTHING SEASONING DIP WITH BAGEL CHIPS

2 large bagels, sliced vertically into rounds

1 container (12 ounces) whipped cream cheese

1½ tablespoons green onion tops, chopped

1 teaspoon minced onion

1 teaspoon minced garlic

1 teaspoon sesame seeds

1 teaspoon poppy seeds

¼ teaspoon kosher salt

1. Preheat air fryer to 350°F.

2. Coat bagel rounds generously with butter-flavored nonstick cooking spray. Cook 7 to 8 minutes or until golden brown, shaking occasionally.

3. Combine cream cheese, green onion, minced onion, garlic, sesame seeds, poppy seeds and salt in medium bowl; stir to blend.

4. Serve chips with dip.

WARM GOAT CHEESE ROUNDS

1 package (4 ounces) garlic herb goat cheese

1 egg

1 tablespoon water

⅓ cup seasoned dry bread crumbs

Marinara sauce

1. Cut cheese crosswise into eight slices. (If cheese is too difficult to slice, shape scant tablespoonfuls of cheese into balls and flatten into ¼-inch-thick rounds.)

2. Beat egg and water in small bowl. Place bread crumbs in shallow dish. Dip cheese rounds into egg mixture, then in bread crumbs, turning to coat all sides. Gently press bread crumbs to adhere. Place coated rounds on plate; freeze 10 minutes.

3. Preheat air fryer to 370°F. Cook in batches 10 minutes, flipping halfway through cooking, until golden brown. Serve immediately with marinara sauce.

PEPPERONI BREAD

1 package (about 14 ounces) refrigerated pizza dough

8 slices provolone cheese

20 to 30 slices pepperoni (about ½ of 6-ounce package)

¾ cup (3 ounces) shredded mozzarella cheese

½ cup grated Parmesan cheese

½ teaspoon Italian seasoning

1 egg, beaten

Marinara sauce, heated

1. Unroll pizza dough on lightly floured surface; cut dough in half.

2. Working with one half at a time, arrange half the provolone slices on half the dough. Top with half the pepperoni, half the mozzarella and Parmesan cheeses and half the Italian seasoning. Repeat with other half bread and toppings.

3. Fold top half of dough over filling; press edges with fork or pinch edges to seal.

4. Preheat air fryer to 390°F. Line basket with parchment paper. Transfer one bread to basket. Brush with egg.

5. Cook 8 to 10 minutes or until crust is golden brown. Remove to wire rack to cool slightly. Repeat with other bread. Cut crosswise into slices; serve warm with marinara sauce.

FALAFEL NUGGETS

SAUCE

- 2½ cups tomato sauce
- ⅓ cup tomato paste
- 2 tablespoons lemon juice
- 2 teaspoons sugar
- 1 teaspoon onion powder
- ½ teaspoon salt

FALAFEL

- 2 cans (about 15 ounces each) chickpeas, rinsed and drained
- ½ cup all-purpose flour
- ½ cup chopped fresh parsley
- 1 egg
- ¼ cup minced onion
- 3 tablespoons lemon juice
- 2 tablespoons minced garlic
- 2 teaspoons ground cumin
- ½ teaspoon salt
- ½ teaspoon ground red pepper or red pepper flakes

1. For sauce, combine tomato sauce, tomato paste, 2 tablespoons lemon juice, sugar, onion powder and ½ teaspoon salt in medium saucepan. Simmer over medium-low heat 20 minutes or until heated through. Cover and keep warm until ready to serve.

2. For falafel, combine chickpeas, flour, parsley, egg, minced onion, 3 tablespoons lemon juice, garlic, cumin, ½ teaspoon salt and ground red pepper in food processor or blender; process until well blended. Shape mixture into 1-inch balls. Spray with nonstick cooking spray.

3. Preheat air fryer to 390°F. Line basket with foil; spray with cooking spray.

4. Cook in batches 12 to 15 minutes, turning halfway through cooking, until browned. Serve with sauce.

FAST-FIXIN' BREAKFASTS

BREAKFAST FLATS

MAKES 4 SERVINGS

1 package (about 14 ounces) refrigerated pizza dough

1½ cups (6 ounces) shredded medium Cheddar cheese

8 slices bacon, crisp-cooked and diced (optional)

4 eggs, fried

Kosher salt and black pepper (optional)

1. Divide pizza dough into four equal portions. Roll out on lightly floured surface into rectangles roughly 8½×4 inches. Top each evenly with cheese and bacon, if desired.

2. Preheat air fryer to 370°F. Line basket with parchment paper.

3. Cook in batches 5 to 7 minutes or until crust is golden brown and crisp and cheese is melted.

4. Top baked flats with fried egg; season with salt and pepper, if desired. Serve warm.

AIR-FRIED OMELET SCRAMBLE

MAKES 1 TO 2 SERVINGS

2 large eggs

2 tablespoons milk

¼ teaspoon salt

⅛ teaspoon black pepper

2 tablespoons chopped red and/or green bell pepper

2 tablespoons chopped onion

¼ cup shredded Cheddar cheese, divided

1. Spray one 6×3-inch baking dish or two small ramekins* with nonstick cooking spray.

2. Whisk eggs, milk, salt and black pepper in medium bowl. Add bell pepper, onion and 2 tablespoons cheese. Pour into prepared dish.

3. Preheat air fryer to 350°F. Cook 10 to 12 minutes slightly breaking up eggs after 5 minutes. Top with remaining cheese.

Depending on the size of your air fryer, you may need to modify the size of the baking dish.

RASPBERRY PUFFS

1 package (8 ounces) refrigerated crescent roll dough

¼ cup raspberry fruit spread

½ of an 8-ounce package cream cheese, softened

1 to 2 teaspoons sugar

2 tablespoons reduced-fat (2%) milk

¼ teaspoon vanilla

1. Separate crescent roll dough into eight triangles; unroll on lightly floured surface. Brush 1½ teaspoons fruit spread evenly over each roll. Roll up each triangle, starting at wide end.

2. Preheat air fryer to 370°F. Line basket with parchment paper.

3. Cook in batches 5 to 6 minutes or until lightly golden. Cool.

4. Meanwhile, whisk together cream cheese, sugar, milk and vanilla in small bowl until smooth. Spoon about 1 tablespoon cream cheese mixture over each cooled roll or serve on the side, as desired.

VARIATION: For an even lighter-tasting roll, replace the cream cheese mixture with powdered sugar. Simply sprinkle 2 tablespoons evenly over all.

OMELET CROISSANTS

2 large croissants

2 large eggs

¼ cup chopped mushrooms

¼ tablespoon chopped red and/or green bell pepper

Pinch each salt and black pepper

¼ cup shredded Cheddar cheese

1. Cut slit across top of each croissant; using hands break open to separate.

2. Whisk eggs in small bowl. Add mushrooms, bell pepper, salt and black pepper. Spoon mixture equally in croissant opening. Sprinkle cheese over top.

3. Preheat air fryer to 330°F. Place croissants in parchment-lined basket.

4. Cook 12 to 15 minutes until croissants are browned and eggs are set.

MAKE AHEAD: Prepared croissants can be stored in refrigerator for up to 3 days or in freezer for 1 month.

CINNAMINI BUNS

MAKES 2 DOZEN

2 tablespoons packed brown sugar

½ teaspoon ground cinnamon

1 package (8 ounces) refrigerated crescent roll dough

1 tablespoon butter, melted

½ cup powdered sugar

1 to 1½ tablespoons milk

1. Combine brown sugar and cinnamon in small bowl; mix well.

2. Unroll dough and separate into two 12×4-inch rectangles; firmly press perforations to seal. Brush dough with butter; sprinkle with brown sugar mixture. Starting with long side, roll up tightly jelly-roll style; pinch seams to seal. Cut each roll crosswise into 12 (1-inch) slices with serrated knife.

3. Preheat air fryer to 370°F. Line basket with parchment paper.

4. Cook, seam side up, in batches 5 to 7 minutes or until golden brown. Remove to wire rack; cool.

5. Combine powdered sugar and 1 tablespoon milk in small bowl; whisk until smooth. Add additional milk, 1 teaspoon at a time, to reach desired glaze consistency. Drizzle glaze over buns.

SAUSAGE ROLLS

MAKES 4 SERVINGS

8 ounces ground pork

¼ cup finely chopped onion

½ teaspoon coarse salt

1 teaspoon minced garlic

½ teaspoon dried thyme

½ teaspoon dried basil

¼ teaspoon dried marjoram

¼ teaspoon black pepper

1 sheet frozen puff pastry (half of 17¼-ounce package), thawed

1 egg, beaten

1. Combine pork, onion, salt, garlic, thyme, basil, marjoram and pepper in medium bowl; mix well.

2. Place puff pastry on floured surface; cut lengthwise into three strips at seams. Roll each third into 10×4½-inch rectangle. Shape one third of pork mixture into 10-inch log; arrange log along top edge of one pastry rectangle. Brush bottom ½ inch of rectangle with egg. Roll pastry down around pork; press to seal. Cut each roll crosswise into four pieces. Repeat with remaining puff pastry and pork mixture. Brush top of each roll with egg.

3. Preheat air fryer to 370°F. Line basket with parchment paper.

4. Cook in batches 8 to 10 minutes or until sausage is cooked through and pastry is golden brown and puffed. Remove to wire rack; cool 10 minutes. Serve warm.

CRUNCHY FRENCH TOAST STICKS

MAKES 6 SERVINGS

6 slices Italian bread (each 1 inch thick, about 3½ to 4 inches in diameter)

4 cups cornflakes, crushed

3 eggs

⅔ cup reduced-fat (2%) milk

1 tablespoon sugar

1 teaspoon vanilla

1 teaspoon ground cinnamon, plus additional for serving

¼ teaspoon ground nutmeg

1 container (6 ounces) vanilla yogurt

¼ cup maple syrup

1. Remove crusts from bread, if desired. Cut each bread slice into three strips. Place cornflakes on waxed paper.

2. Whisk eggs, milk, sugar, vanilla, 1 teaspoon cinnamon and nutmeg in shallow dish. Dip bread strips in egg mixture, turning to generously coat all sides. Roll in cornflakes, coating all sides.

3. Preheat air fryer to 370°F. Cook in batches 8 to 10 minutes, turning halfway through cooking or until golden brown.

4. Meanwhile, combine yogurt and maple syrup in small bowl. Sprinkle with additional cinnamon, if desired. Serve French toast sticks with yogurt mixture.

QUICK JELLY-FILLED BISCUIT DOUGHNUT BALLS

MAKES 20 DOUGHNUT BALLS

1 package (about 7 ounces) refrigerated reduced-fat biscuit dough (10 biscuits)

¼ cup coarse sugar

1 cup strawberry preserves*

If preserves are very chunky, process in food processor 10 seconds or press through fine-mesh sieve.

1. Preheat air fryer to 370°F.

2. Separate biscuits into 10 portions. Cut each in half; roll dough into balls to create 20 balls.

3. Cook in batches 5 to 6 minutes or until golden brown.

4. Place sugar in large bowl. Coat warm balls in sugar. Let cool. Using a piping bag with medium star tip; fill bag with preserves. Poke hole in side of each doughnut ball with paring knife; fill with preserves. Serve immediately.

BREAKFAST BURRITOS

MAKES 4 SERVINGS

4 turkey breakfast sausage links

2 eggs

½ teaspoon ground cumin (optional)

4 (6-inch) yellow or white corn tortillas

¼ cup prepared salsa

1. Preheat air fryer to 370°F. Line basket with parchment paper.

2. Cook sausages 6 to 8 minutes or until browned on the outside and cooked through, shaking occasionally during cooking. Remove sausages to plate.

3. Whisk eggs and cumin, if desired, in small bowl. Heat small skillet over medium-high heat. Cook eggs until done.

4. Place sausage link in middle of each tortilla. Spoon equal amounts of scrambled egg on top of sausage. Roll up to enclose the filling; secure with toothpicks.

5. Cook in air fryer 2 to 3 minutes or until heated through.

6. Pour salsa in small bowl. Serve with burritos.

RASPBERRY WHITE CHOCOLATE DANISH

MAKES 8 SERVINGS

1 package (8 ounces) refrigerated crescent roll dough

8 teaspoons red raspberry preserves

1 ounce white baking chocolate, chopped

1. Unroll crescent dough; separate into eight triangles. Place 1 teaspoon preserves in center of each triangle. Fold right and left corners of long side over filling to top corner to form rectangle. Pinch edges to seal.

2. Preheat air fryer to 370°F. Line basket with parchment paper; spray with nonstick cooking spray.

3. Cook, seam side up, in batches 5 to 7 minutes or until lightly browned. Remove to wire rack to cool 5 minutes.

4. Place white chocolate in small resealable food storage bag. Microwave on MEDIUM (50%) 1 minute; gently knead bag. Microwave and knead at additional 30-second intervals until chocolate is completely melted. Cut off small corner of bag; drizzle chocolate over danish.

FRENCH TOAST STICKS

4 eggs

⅓ cup reduced-fat (2%) milk

1 teaspoon ground cinnamon

1 teaspoon vanilla

4 slices Italian bread, cut into 3 portions each

1 teaspoon powdered sugar

¼ cup maple syrup

1. Combine eggs, milk, cinnamon and vanilla in large shallow dish.

2. Dip bread sticks in egg mixture to coat.

3. Preheat air fryer to 370°F. Line basket with parchment paper; spray with nonstick cooking spray.

4. Cook in batches 8 to 10 minutes or until golden brown. Dust lightly with powdered sugar; serve with maple syrup.

CAULIFLOWER "HASH BROWN" PATTIES

MAKES 8 SERVINGS

4 slices bacon

1 package (about 12 ounces) cauliflower rice

½ cup finely chopped onion

½ cup finely chopped red and/or green bell pepper

1 large egg

⅓ cup all-purpose flour or almond flour

½ cup (2 ounces) shredded Cheddar cheese

1 tablespoon chopped fresh chives

1 teaspoon salt

½ teaspoon black pepper

1. Preheat air fryer to 400°F. Cook bacon 8 to 10 minutes. Remove from basket to paper towels; blot any grease from bacon. Crumble into small pieces.

2. Place cauliflower in large bowl. Add bacon, onion, bell pepper, egg, flour, cheese, chives, salt and black pepper; mix well. Shape mixture into patties; place on baking sheet. Freeze 30 minutes.

3. Preheat air fryer to 370°F. Spray basket with nonstick cooking spray. Cook 12 to 15 minutes or until browned.

HOMEMADE AIR-FRIED BAGELS

MAKES 4 SERVINGS

1 cup self-rising flour

1 cup nonfat plain Greek yogurt

1 large egg, beaten

Sesame seeds, poppy seeds, dried onion flakes, everything bagel seasoning (optional)

Cream cheese or butter

1. Combine flour and yogurt in bowl of electric stand mixer with dough hook.* Beat 2 to 3 minutes or until mixture is well combined. Place dough on lightly floured surface; knead by hand about 4 to 5 minutes or until dough is smooth and elastic. Form dough into a ball.

2. Cut into four equal portions. Roll each into a ball. Pull and stretch dough to create desired shape, inserting finger into center to create hole. Repeat with remaining dough.

3. Preheat air fryer to 330°F. Line basket with parchment paper. Place bagels on parchment; brush with egg wash. Sprinkle with desired toppings. Cook 8 to 10 minutes or until lightly browned.

4. Serve with cream cheese or butter.

Or, use heavy spatula in large bowl to combine mixture.

BISCUIT-WRAPPED SAUSAGES

MAKES 6 SERVINGS

1 package (8 ounces) refrigerated crescent dough sheet

1 package (about 12 ounces) fully cooked breakfast sausage links

Maple syrup (optional)

1. Unroll crescent dough; cut dough into thin strips. Wrap each sausage link with dough. Insert wooden skewers through sausages.*

2. Preheat air fryer to 370°F.

3. Cook 5 to 7 minutes or until golden brown. Cool slightly; remove to large serving platter. Serve with maple syrup for dipping.

Soak wooden skewers 20 minutes in cool water. Depending on the size of your air fryer, you may need to shorten the skewers to fit.

LIGHT LUNCHES

AIR-FRIED PEPPERONI PIZZA BAGELS

4 **Homemade Air-Fried Bagels (recipe on page 60) or store bought bagels**

¼ **cup marinara sauce**

¼ **cup mini pepperoni slices**

¼ **cup shredded mozzarella cheese**

Dried oregano

1. Cut bagels in half lengthwise. Top each with equal amount sauce, pepperoni and cheese.

2. Preheat air fryer to 350°F. Line basket with foil or parchment paper. Cook 3 to 5 minutes or until cheese is melted and browned. Sprinkle with oregano.

SPINACH & ROASTED PEPPER PANINI

1 loaf (12 ounces) focaccia

1½ cups spinach leaves
(about 12 leaves)

1 jar (about 7 ounces)
roasted red peppers,
drained

4 ounces fontina cheese,
thinly sliced

¾ cup thinly sliced red onion

Olive oil

1. Cut focaccia in half horizontally. Layer bottom half with spinach, peppers, cheese and onion. Cover with top half of focaccia. Brush outsides of sandwich lightly with oil. Cut sandwich into four equal pieces.

2. Preheat air fryer to 370°F. Line basket with parchment paper. Cook in batches 3 to 5 minutes or until cheese melts and bread is golden brown.

NOTE: Focaccia can be found in the bakery section of most supermarkets. It is often available in different flavors, such as tomato, herb, cheese or onion.

PECAN-CRUSTED CHICKEN SALAD

MAKES 4 SERVINGS

CHICKEN

- ½ cup all-purpose flour
- ½ cup milk
- 1 egg
- ⅔ cup cornflake crumbs
- ⅔ cup finely chopped pecans
- ¾ teaspoon salt
- 4 boneless skinless chicken breasts (1¼-1½ pounds total)

SALAD

- 10 cups mixed greens (1-pound package)
- 2 cans (11 ounces each) mandarin oranges, drained
- 1 cup sliced celery
- ¾ cup dried cranberries
- ½ cup glazed pecans*
- ½ cup crumbled blue cheese
- ¾ cup prepared balsamic salad dressing or other dressing of choice

Glazed or candied pecans or walnuts are often found in the produce section of the supermarket along with other salad convenience items.

1. For chicken, place flour in shallow dish. Beat milk and egg in another shallow dish. Combine cornflake crumbs, chopped pecans and salt in third shallow dish. Dip both sides of chicken in flour, then in egg mixture, letting excess drip back into dish. Roll in crumb mixture to coat completely, pressing crumbs into chicken to adhere.

2. Preheat air fryer to 390°F. Line basket with foil; spray with nonstick cooking spray.

3. Cook in batches 18 to 20 minutes or until chicken is no longer pink in center. Cool completely before slicing. (Chicken can be prepared several hours in advance and refrigerated.)

4. For salad, combine mixed greens, mandarin oranges, celery, cranberries, glazed pecans and cheese in large bowl. Toss gently with ¼ cup salad dressing to coat. Divide salad among four plates. Cut chicken breasts diagonally into ½-inch slices; arrange over salads. Serve with remaining dressing.

SALMON CROQUETTES

MAKES 5 SERVINGS

1 can (14¾ ounces) pink salmon, drained and flaked

½ cup mashed potatoes*

1 egg, beaten

3 tablespoons diced red bell pepper

2 tablespoons sliced green onion

1 tablespoon chopped fresh parsley

½ cup seasoned dry bread crumbs

Use mashed potatoes that are freshly made, leftover, or potatoes made from instant potatoes.

1. Combine salmon, potatoes, egg, bell pepper, green onion and parsley in medium bowl; mix well.

2. Place bread crumbs on medium plate. Shape salmon mixture into 10 croquettes about 3 inches long by 1 inch wide. Roll croquettes in crumbs to coat. Refrigerate 15 to 20 minutes or until firm.

3. Preheat air fryer to 350°F. Cook in batches 6 to 8 minutes or until browned. Serve immediately.

PESTO, RAMEN AND CHEESE SANDWICH

MAKES 4 SERVINGS

1 package (3 ounces) ramen noodles, any flavor*

¼ cup prepared pesto

8 slices French or Italian bread

4 slices provolone cheese

1 tomato, cut into slices

3 tablespoons butter, melted

Discard seasoning packet.

1. Prepare ramen noodles according to package directions; rinse and drain well. Place noodles in medium bowl; add pesto, stirring to mix well.

2. Divide noodle mixture among four bread slices. Evenly top with cheese, tomato and remaining bread slices. Brush sandwiches with butter.

3. Preheat air fryer to 350°F. Cook in batches 3 to 4 minutes on each side or until cheese melts and bread is golden brown.

BACON-TOMATO GRILLED CHEESE

MAKES 2 SERVINGS

4 slices bacon, cut in half

2 slices sharp Cheddar cheese

2 slices Gouda cheese

2 slices tomato

4 slices whole wheat or white bread

1. Preheat air fryer to 400°F. Cook bacon 8 to 10 minutes. Remove from basket to paper towels; blot any grease from bacon.

2. Meanwhile, layer 1 slice of Cheddar cheese, 1 slice of Gouda cheese, 1 tomato slice and 2 slices bacon between 2 bread slices. Repeat with remaining ingredients.

3. Cook 3 to 5 minutes or until cheese is melted and bread is golden brown.

BAKED SALAMI

1 all-beef kosher salami (14 to 16 ounces)

½ cup apricot preserves

1 tablespoon hot pepper sauce

2 tablespoons packed brown sugar

Bread slices

1. Peel off plastic wrap of salami. Cut 12 crosswise (½-inch-deep) slits across top. Place, cut side up, in small dish that fits inside air fryer.

2. Combine preserves, hot pepper sauce and brown sugar in small bowl; stir well. Spoon sauce over top.

3. Preheat air fryer to 370°F. Cook 8 to 10 minutes or until juicy and dark brown, spooning sauce over salami occasionally during cooking.

4. Cut salami into thin slices; toss with sauce. Serve on bread.

EXTRAS: Serve with slices of challah bread or cocktail rye.

TASTY TURKEY TURNOVERS

1 package (about 8 ounces) refrigerated crescent roll sheet

2 tablespoons honey mustard, plus additional for serving

3 ounces thinly sliced lean deli turkey breast

¾ cup packaged broccoli coleslaw

1 egg white, beaten

1. Roll out dough on lightly floured surface. Using a wide glass or cookie cutter, cut into 3½-inch circles. Spread 2 tablespoons honey mustard lightly over dough circles; top with turkey and coleslaw. Brush edges of dough with beaten egg white. Fold circles in half; press edges with tines of fork to seal. Brush with egg white.

2. Preheat air fryer to 370°F. Spray basket with nonstick cooking spray.

3. Cook in batches 6 to 7 minutes or until golden brown. Let stand 5 minutes before serving. Serve warm or at room temperature with additional honey mustard for dipping, if desired.

FISH BITES WITH ROMESCO SAUCE

MAKES 4 SERVINGS

1 jar (12 ounces) roasted red peppers, drained

4 plum tomatoes, quartered

½ cup raw almonds

2 cloves garlic, peeled

¼ cup fresh parsley

1 tablespoon olive oil

1 tablespoon lemon juice

½ teaspoon salt, divided

2 egg whites

¼ cup all-purpose flour

½ teaspoon ground red pepper

¼ cup ground almonds

½ pound tilapia fillets, cut into 1-inch pieces

1. For sauce, place roasted red peppers, tomatoes, raw almonds, garlic, parsley, oil, lemon juice and ¼ teaspoon salt in food processor; process using on/off pulsing action just until ingredients are almost smooth. Place sauce in small bowl; set aside.

2. Lightly beat egg whites in small bowl. Combine flour, ground red pepper and remaining ¼ teaspoon salt in shallow dish. Place ground almonds in second shallow dish.

3. Coat fish in flour mixture, shaking off excess. Dip into egg whites; roll in ground almonds until evenly coated.

4. Preheat air fryer to 390°F. Lightly spray basket with nonstick cooking spray.

5. Cook in batches 8 to 10 minutes or until golden brown and fish begins to flake when tested with fork. Serve immediately with sauce.

PIZZA SANDWICH

MAKES 4 TO 6 SERVINGS

1 loaf (12 ounces) focaccia

½ cup pizza sauce

20 slices pepperoni

8 slices (1 ounce each) mozzarella cheese

1 can (2¼ ounces) sliced mushrooms, drained

Red pepper flakes (optional)

Olive oil

1. Cut focaccia horizontally in half. Spread cut sides of both halves with pizza sauce. Layer bottom half with pepperoni, cheese and mushrooms; sprinkle with red pepper flakes, if desired. Cover with top half of focaccia. Brush sandwich lightly with oil.*

2. Preheat air fryer to 370°F.

3. Cook 3 to 5 minutes or until cheese melts and bread is golden brown. Cut into wedges to serve.

Depending on the size of your air fryer, you may need to cut the focaccia vertically in half to fit.

NOTE: Focaccia can be found in the bakery section of most supermarkets. It is often available in different flavors, such as tomato, herb, cheese or onion.

QUICK DINNERS

EASY AIR-FRIED CHICKEN THIGHS

MAKES 4 SERVINGS

8 bone-in or boneless chicken thighs with skin

1 teaspoon garlic powder

1 teaspoon onion powder

1 teaspoon dried oregano

1 teaspoon ground thyme

1 teaspoon paprika

1 teaspoon salt

1 teaspoon black pepper

1. Place chicken in large resealable food storage bag. Combine garlic powder, onion powder, oregano, thyme, paprika, salt and pepper in small bowl; mix well. Add to chicken; shake until spices are distributed.

2. Preheat air fryer to 350°F. Line basket with parchment paper; spray with nonstick cooking spray.

3. Cook in batches 20 to 25 minutes until golden browned and cooked throughout, turning chicken halfway through cooking.

NOTE: Try this chicken with other favorite spices as well.

TERIYAKI SALMON

¼ cup dark sesame oil

Juice of 1 lemon

¼ cup soy sauce

2 tablespoons packed brown sugar

1 clove garlic, minced

2 salmon fillets (about 4 ounces each)

Hot cooked rice

Toasted sesame seeds and green onions (optional)

1. Whisk oil, lemon juice, soy sauce, brown sugar and garlic in medium bowl. Place salmon in large resealable food storage bag; add marinade. Refrigerate at least 2 hours.

2. Preheat air fryer to 350°F. Spray basket with nonstick cooking spray.

3. Cook 8 to 10 minutes until salmon is crispy and easily flakes when tested with a fork. Serve with rice and garnish as desired.

BUTTERMILK AIR-FRIED CHICKEN

1 cut-up whole chicken
(2½ to 3 pounds)

1 cup buttermilk

¾ cup all-purpose flour

½ teaspoon salt

½ teaspoon ground red
pepper

¼ teaspoon garlic powder

2 cups plain dry bread
crumbs

1. Place chicken pieces in large resealable food storage bag. Pour buttermilk over chicken. Close and refrigerate; let marinate at least 2 hours.

2. Combine flour, salt, ground red pepper and garlic powder in large shallow bowl. Place bread crumbs in another shallow bowl.

3. Preheat air fryer to 390°F. Spray basket with nonstick cooking spray.

4. Remove chicken pieces from buttermilk; coat with flour mixture then coat in bread crumbs. Spray chicken with cooking spray. Cook 20 to 25 minutes or until brown and crisp on all sides and cooked through (165°F). Serve warm.

CAULIFLOWER TACOS WITH CHIPOTLE CREMA

- 1 package (8 ounces) sliced cremini mushrooms
- 4 tablespoons olive oil, divided
- 1¾ teaspoons salt, divided
- 1 head cauliflower
- 1 teaspoon ground cumin
- ½ teaspoon dried oregano
- ¼ teaspoon ground coriander
- ¼ teaspoon ground cinnamon
- ¼ teaspoon black pepper
- ½ cup sour cream
- 2 teaspoons lime juice
- ½ teaspoon chipotle chili powder
- ½ cup vegetarian refried beans
- 8 taco-size flour or corn tortillas
- Chopped fresh cilantro (optional)
- Pickled Red Onions (recipe follows) or chopped red onion

1. Toss mushrooms with 1 tablespoon oil and ¼ teaspoon salt in large bowl.

2. Remove leaves from cauliflower. Cut florets into 1-inch pieces; place in large bowl. Add remaining 3 tablespoons olive oil, 1 teaspoon salt, cumin, oregano, coriander, cinnamon and black pepper; toss well.

3. Preheat air fryer to 390°F. Spray basket with nonstick cooking spray. Cook cauliflower 8 to 10 minutes or until browned and tender, shaking occasionally. Remove to large bowl.

4. Add mushrooms to basket. Cook 6 to 8 minutes or until browned, shaking occasionally.

5. For crema, combine sour cream, lime juice, chili powder and remaining ½ teaspoon salt in small bowl.

6. For each taco, spread 1 tablespoon beans and 1 teaspoon crema over each tortilla. Top with about 3 mushroom slices and ¼ cup cauliflower. Top with cilantro and red onions, if desired. Fold in half.

PICKLED RED ONIONS: Thinly slice 1 small red onion; place in large glass jar. Add ¼ cup white wine vinegar or distilled white vinegar, 2 tablespoons water, 1 teaspoon sugar and 1 teaspoon salt. Seal jar; shake well. Refrigerate at least 1 hour or up to 1 week. Makes about ½ cup.

COCONUT SHRIMP

DIPPING SAUCE

- ½ **cup orange marmalade**
- ⅓ **cup Thai chili sauce**
- 1 **teaspoon prepared horseradish**
- ½ **teaspoon salt**

SHRIMP

- 1 **cup flat beer**
- 1 **cup all-purpose flour**
- 2 **cups sweetened flaked coconut, divided**
- 2 **tablespoons sugar**
- 16 **to 20 large raw shrimp, peeled and deveined (with tails on), patted dry**

1. For dipping sauce, combine marmalade, chili sauce, horseradish and salt in small bowl; mix well. Cover and refrigerate until ready to serve.

2. For shrimp, whisk beer, flour, ½ cup coconut and sugar in large bowl until well blended. Place remaining 1½ cups coconut in medium bowl.

3. Preheat air fryer to 390°F. Line basket with parchment paper; spray with nonstick cooking spray.

4. Dip shrimp in beer batter, then in coconut, turning to coat completely. Cook in batches 5 to 7 minutes, turning halfway through cooking, until golden brown. Serve with dipping sauce.

CRISPY CRAB CAKES WITH MANGO SALSA

MAKES 24 APPETIZER CAKES

- 1 cup plain dry bread crumbs, divided
- ¼ cup mayonnaise
- 1 large egg, beaten
- 1 tablespoon Dijon mustard
- 2 tablespoons chopped green onion, white and green parts
- ½ teaspoon Worcestershire sauce
- ½ teaspoon seafood seasoning
- ½ teaspoon salt
- ½ teaspoon black pepper
- 1 pound fresh lump crabmeat, picked over for cartilage
- Mango Salsa (recipe follows)

1. Combine ½ cup bread crumbs, mayonnaise, egg, mustard, green onion, Worcestershire sauce, seafood seasoning, salt and pepper in large bowl; stir in crabmeat. Using wet hands, form mixture into patties. Place on parchment-lined baking sheet; refrigerate at least 30 minutes.

2. Place remaining ½ cup bread crumbs in shallow dish. Roll patties in bread crumbs, coating well. Prepare Mango Salsa.

3. Preheat air fryer to 370°F. Line basket with parchment paper. Cook in batches 8 to 10 minutes until golden brown, flipping halfway through cooking. Serve with Mango Salsa.

MANGO SALSA

2 cups chopped mango

2 jalapeño peppers,* seeded and diced

1 cup chopped red bell pepper

⅔ cup chopped green onions

¼ cup chopped fresh cilantro

2 tablespoons fresh lime juice

1 tablespoon vegetable oil

Salt and black pepper

**Jalapeño peppers can sting and irritate the skin, so wear rubber gloves when handling peppers and do not touch your eyes.

Mix all ingredients in small bowl. Season to taste with salt and black pepper. (Can be made ahead. Cover and chill.)

PARMESAN-CRUSTED TILAPIA

- ⅔ cup plus 3 tablespoons grated Parmesan cheese, divided
- ⅔ cup panko bread crumbs
- ⅓ cup prepared Alfredo sauce (refrigerated or jarred)
- 1½ teaspoons dried parsley flakes
- 4 tilapia fillets (6 ounces each)
- Shaved Parmesan cheese (optional)
- Minced fresh parsley (optional)

1. Combine ⅔ cup grated cheese and panko in medium bowl; mix well. Combine Alfredo sauce, remaining 3 tablespoons grated cheese and parsley flakes in small bowl; mix well. Spread mixture over top of fish, coating in thick even layer. Top with panko mixture, pressing in gently to adhere.

2. Preheat air fryer to 390°F. Line basket with foil or parchment paper; spray with nonstick cooking spray.

3. Cook in batches 8 to 10 minutes or until crust is golden brown and fish begins to flake when tested with a fork. Garnish with shaved Parmesan and fresh parsley.

CHICKEN AIR-FRIED STEAK WITH CREAMY GRAVY

MAKES 4 TO 6 SERVINGS

- ½ cup all-purpose flour
- ½ teaspoon kosher salt
- ½ teaspoon onion powder
- ¼ teaspoon paprika
- ¼ teaspoon ground red pepper
- ⅛ teaspoon black pepper
- 1 large egg
- ¼ cup water

- 1 pound cube steak, divided into 4 to 6 portions

GRAVY
- 1½ tablespoons butter
- 2 to 3 tablespoons all-purpose flour
- ¾ cup chicken broth
- ½ cup milk
- Salt and black pepper

1. Combine ½ cup flour, kosher salt, onion powder, paprika, ground red pepper and black pepper in shallow dish. Whisk egg and water in another shallow dish.

2. Dredge steaks in flour mixture, then egg mixture, letting excess drain back into dish, then again in flour mixture to coat well.

3. Preheat air fryer to 370°F. Spray basket with nonstick cooking spray or line with parchment paper sprayed with cooking spray.

4. Cook in batches 12 to 14 minutes, turning halfway through cooking, until steaks are browned and no longer pink in middle. Remove to serving plate.

5. For gravy, melt butter in small skillet over medium heat. Add 2 tablespoons flour, broth and milk. Cook and stir until slightly thickened. If necessary, add additional 1 tablespoon flour to thicken. Season with salt and black pepper. Serve steaks with gravy.

FRIED GREEN TOMATO PARMESAN

MAKES 2 SERVINGS

1 can (15 ounces) no-salt-added tomato sauce, divided

2 green tomatoes

Salt and black pepper

¼ cup all-purpose flour

½ teaspoon Italian seasoning

1 egg

1 tablespoon water

¾ cup panko bread crumbs

¼ cup shredded Parmesan cheese

Shredded fresh basil

Hot cooked spaghetti (optional)

1. Spread ½ cup tomato sauce in small baking dish that fits inside air fryer basket.

2. Cut tomatoes into ¼-inch slices. Lightly season with salt and pepper, if desired.

3. Combine flour, Italian seasoning and ⅛ teaspoon salt, if desired, in shallow dish. Whisk egg and water in another shallow bowl. Place panko in third shallow bowl. Coat tomatoes with flour mixture. Dip in egg mixture. Dredge in panko, pressing onto all sides.

4. Preheat air fryer to 350°F. Cook in batches 2 to 3 minutes per side or until panko is golden brown. Remove tomatoes to sauce in baking dish, slightly overlapping. Sprinkle with Parmesan cheese and ½ cup tomato sauce.

5. Cook 6 to 8 minutes or until cheese is melted and sauce is heated through. Sprinkle with basil. Serve with spaghetti, if desired, and remaining tomato sauce.

LEMON PEPPER CHICKEN

⅓ cup lemon juice

¼ cup finely chopped onion

¼ cup olive oil

1 tablespoon packed brown sugar

1 tablespoon black pepper

3 cloves garlic, minced

2 teaspoons grated lemon peel

¾ teaspoon salt

4 boneless skinless chicken breasts

1. Combine lemon juice, onion, oil, brown sugar, pepper, garlic, lemon peel and salt in small bowl. Pour marinade over chicken in large resealable food storage bag. Seal bag; knead to coat. Refrigerate at least 4 hours or overnight.

2. Preheat air fryer to 370°F. Line basket with parchment paper.

3. Remove chicken from marinade; discard marinade. Cook in batches 15 to 20 minutes or until chicken is browned and no longer pink in center.

CAPRESE PORTOBELLOS

MAKES 4 SERVINGS

2 tablespoons butter

½ teaspoon minced garlic

1 teaspoon dried parsley flakes

4 portobello mushrooms, stems removed

1 cup (4 ounces) shredded mozzarella cheese

1 cup cherry or grape tomatoes, thinly sliced

2 tablespoons fresh basil, thinly sliced

Balsamic glaze

1. Combine butter, garlic and parsley flakes in small dish. Microwave on LOW 30 seconds or until melted.

2. Wash mushrooms thoroughly; dry on paper towels. Brush both sides of mushrooms with butter mixture.

3. Preheat air fryer to 390°F. Spray basket with nonstick cooking spray.

4. Fill mushroom caps with about ¼ cup cheese each. Top with sliced tomatoes. Cook 5 to 7 minutes or until cheese is melted and lightly browned. Top with basil.

5. Drizzle with balsamic glaze before serving.

AIR-FRIED FRIES

2 small russet potatoes (10 ounces), refrigerated

2 teaspoons olive oil

¼ teaspoon salt or onion salt

1. Peel potatoes and cut lengthwise into ¼-inch strips. Place in colander; rinse under cold running water 2 minutes. Drain. Pat dry with paper towels.

2. Place potatoes in large resealable food storage bag. Drizzle with oil. Seal bag; shake to coat evenly.

3. Preheat air fryer to 390°F. Cook 15 to 18 minutes, shaking occasionally during cooking, until light brown and crisp. Sprinkle with salt.

NOTE: Refrigerating potatoes—usually not recommended for storage—converts the starch in the potatoes to sugar, which enhances the browning when the potatoes are baked. Do not refrigerate the potatoes longer than 2 days, because they may develop a sweet flavor.

ZUCCHINI FRITTE

Lemon Aioli (recipe follows)

¾ to 1 cup soda water

½ cup all-purpose flour

¼ cup cornstarch

½ teaspoon coarse salt, plus additional for serving

¼ teaspoon garlic powder

¼ teaspoon dried oregano

¼ teaspoon black pepper

3 cups panko bread crumbs

1½ pounds medium zucchini (about 8 inches long), ends trimmed, cut lengthwise into ¼-inch-thick slices

¼ cup grated Parmesan or Romano cheese

Chopped fresh parsley

Lemon wedges

1. Prepare Lemon Aioli; cover and refrigerate until ready to use.

2. Pour ¾ cup soda water into large bowl. Combine flour, cornstarch, ½ teaspoon salt, garlic powder, oregano and pepper in medium bowl; mix well. Gradually whisk flour mixture into soda water just until blended. Add additional soda water, if necessary, to reach consistency of thin pancake batter. Place panko in shallow dish.

3. Working with one at a time, dip zucchini slices into batter to coat; let excess batter drip back into bowl. Add to panko; pressing into zucchini slices to coat both sides completely.

4. Preheat air fryer to 390°F. Line basket with parchment paper.

5. Cook in batches 7 to 10 minutes or until golden brown. Sprinkle with cheese and parsley. Serve with Lemon Aioli and lemon wedges.

LEMON AIOLI: Combine ½ cup mayonnaise, 2 tablespoons lemon juice, 1 tablespoon chopped fresh Italian parsley and 1 clove minced garlic in small bowl; mix well. Season with salt and pepper.

AIR-FRIED CORN-ON-THE-COB

MAKES 2 SERVINGS

2 teaspoons butter, melted

¼ teaspoon salt

½ teaspoon black pepper

½ teaspoon chopped fresh parsley

2 ears corn, husks and silks removed

Foil

Grated Parmesan cheese (optional)

1. Combine butter, salt, pepper and parsley in small bowl. Brush corn with butter mixture. Wrap each ear of corn in foil.*

2. Preheat air fryer to 390°F. Cook 10 to 12 minutes, turning halfway through cooking. Sprinkle with Parmesan cheese before serving, if desired.

If your air fryer basket is on the smaller side, you may need to break ears of corn in half to fit.

ZUCCHINI TOMATO ROUNDS

2 large zucchini

Foil

½ cup cherry tomatoes, sliced

1 tablespoon olive oil

2 cloves garlic, minced

2 teaspoons Italian seasoning

1 teaspoon grated Parmesan cheese

1. Cut zucchini into thin slices three-fourths of the way down (do not cut all the way through). Place zucchini on foil sprayed with nonstick cooking spray.

2. Place tomato slices between each zucchini slice. Combine oil and garlic in small bowl. Drizzle over zucchini. Sprinkle with Italian seasoning and cheese. Wrap foil around zucchini.

3. Preheat air fryer to 390°F. Place foil packets in basket. Cook 10 to 12 minutes or until browned and softened.

SWEET POTATO FRIES

2 sweet potatoes, peeled and sliced

1 tablespoon olive oil

¼ teaspoon coarse salt

¼ teaspoon black pepper

½ cup grated Parmesan cheese (optional)

1. Toss potatoes with oil, salt and pepper in medium bowl.

2. Preheat air fryer to 390°F. Spray basket with nonstick cooking spray.

3. Cook 10 to 12 minutes, shaking occasionally during cooking, until lightly browned. Sprinkle with Parmesan cheese, if desired.

CHEESY GARLIC BREAD

MAKES 4 TO 6 SERVINGS

1 loaf (about 8 ounces) Italian bread

¼ cup (½ stick) butter, softened

4 cloves garlic, diced

2 tablespoons grated Parmesan cheese

1 cup (4 ounces) shredded mozzarella cheese

1. Cut bread in half horizontally. Spread cut sides of bread evenly with butter; top with garlic. Sprinkle with Parmesan, then mozzarella cheeses.

2. Preheat air fryer to 370°F. Line basket with foil.

3. Cook 5 to 6 minutes or until cheeses are melted and golden brown. Cut crosswise into slices. Serve warm.

POTATO BALLS

2 cups refrigerated leftover mashed potatoes*

2 tablespoons flour, plus additional for rolling balls

⅔ cup shredded Cheddar cheese

¼ cup chopped green onions

1 large egg

½ teaspoon salt

¼ teaspoon black pepper

1½ cups dry Italian bread crumbs

If you don't have leftover potatoes, prepare 2 cups instant mashed potatoes and refrigerate at least 1 hour.

1. Combine potatoes, 2 tablespoons flour, cheese and green onions in large bowl. Scoop out about 2 tablespoons mixture and roll into a 1-inch ball, adding additional flour, if necessary, making about 18 to 20 balls.

2. Beat egg, salt and pepper in medium bowl. Place bread crumbs in shallow dish. Dip balls in egg, then in bread crumbs until fully coated. Place on baking sheet; refrigerate 30 minutes.

3. Preheat air fryer to 390°F. Spray basket with nonstick cooking spray.

4. Cook in batches 8 to 10 minutes or until balls are browned and heated through.

GRILLED EGGPLANT ROLL-UPS

4 slices Grilled Eggplant (recipe follows)

¼ cup hummus

¼ cup crumbled feta cheese

¼ cup chopped green onions

4 tomato slices, cut in half

1. Prepare Grilled Eggplant. Spread 1 tablespoon hummus on each eggplant slice. Top with 1 tablespoon feta cheese, 1 tablespoon green onions and 2 tomato halves.

2. Roll up tightly. Serve immediately.

GRILLED EGGPLANT: Preheat air fryer to 350°F. Spray basket with nonstick cooking spray. Sprinkle four 1-inch-thick eggplant slices with ½ teaspoon salt; let stand 15 minutes. Brush eggplant with olive oil. Cook in batches 5 minutes; turn and brush with olive oil. Cook 5 minutes or until tender.

CURLY AIR-FRIED FRIES

2 large russet potatoes, unpeeled

¼ cup finely chopped onion

1 teaspoon vegetable oil

½ teaspoon salt

¼ teaspoon black pepper

Honey mustard dipping sauce, ketchup or other favorite dipping sauce

1. Spiral potatoes with thick spiral blade of spiralizer.*

2. Place potatoes and onion in large bowl; drizzle with oil. Toss well.

3. Preheat air fryer to 390°F. Line basket with parchment paper. Cook 12 to 15 minutes or until golden brown and crispy, shaking occasionally during cooking. Sprinkle with salt and pepper.

4. Serve with dipping sauce.

*If you do not have a spiralizer, cut potatoes into thin strips.

FUN FOR KIDS

PIGGIES IN A BASKET

MAKES 4 SERVINGS

1 package (8 ounces) refrigerated crescent roll dough

1 package (about 12 ounces) cocktail franks

1. Cut crescent dough into strips. Wrap dough around each frank.

2. Preheat air fryer to 350°F.

3. Cook in batches 3 to 4 minutes or until golden brown.

CINNAMON TOAST POPPERS

MAKES 12 SERVINGS

6 cups fresh bread* cubes
(1-inch cubes)

2 tablespoons butter, melted

1 tablespoon plus
1½ teaspoons sugar

½ teaspoon ground
cinnamon

*Use a firm sourdough, whole
wheat or semolina bread.*

1. Place bread cubes in large bowl. Drizzle with butter; toss to coat.

2. Combine sugar and cinnamon in small bowl. Sprinkle over bread cubes; mix well.

3. Preheat air fryer to 350°F. Cook 10 to 12 minutes, shaking occasionally during cooking, until bread is golden and fragrant. Serve warm or at room temperature.

BIG KID SHRIMP

MAKES 4 SERVINGS

½ cup plain dry bread crumbs

¼ cup grated Parmesan cheese

½ teaspoon paprika

½ teaspoon salt

⅛ teaspoon black pepper

2 tablespoons butter, melted

1 pound large raw shrimp, peeled and deveined (with tails on)

½ cup mayonnaise

½ cup ketchup

1 tablespoon sweet pickle relish

1. Combine bread crumbs, Parmesan cheese, paprika, salt and pepper in large bowl. Add butter; mix well. Rinse shrimp under cold water, drain. Toss with bread crumb mixture.

2. Preheat air fryer to 390°F. Line basket with parchment paper; spray with nonstick cooking spray.

3. Cook 5 to 7 minutes or until lightly browned and cooked through.

4. Combine mayonnaise, ketchup and relish in small bowl. Serve with shrimp.

TUNA PIES

- 1 package (8 ounces) refrigerated crescent dough sheet
- 1 can (about 5 ounces) water-packed tuna, drained
- 1 tablespoon mayonnaise
- 1 cup (4 ounces) shredded Cheddar cheese

1. Preheat air fryer to 370°F. Spray four ramekins with nonstick cooking spray.

2. Roll out dough onto lightly floured surface to 12×8-inch rectangle. Cut into four 6×4-inch rectangles. Press dough into bottoms and up sides of prepared ramekins.

3. Combine tuna and mayonnaise in small bowl; mix gently. Spoon tuna mixture evenly over dough; sprinkle with cheese.

4. Cook in batches 8 to 10 minutes or until dough is golden brown. Let cool slightly before serving.

VARIATION: You can add your favorite vegetables, like broccoli or peas, to this recipe, as well as trying other types of cheese, like mozzarella or Swiss.

BANANA BOWTIES

MAKES 20 BOWTIES

1 cup peeled chopped ripe
   banana (about 2 medium)

¼ cup finely chopped
   walnuts or pecans

1 tablespoon packed brown
   sugar

20 square wonton wrappers

1 egg, beaten

Chocolate syrup

1. Combine banana, nuts and brown sugar in small bowl; gently mix.

2. Arrange wonton wrappers, one at a time, on clean surface. Brush edges with egg. Place teaspoonful of banana filling in center. Fold wrapper in half, pressing edges to seal. Pinch center to form bowtie. Cover with plastic wrap and refrigerate until needed. Repeat with remaining wrappers and filling.

3. Preheat air fryer to 370°F.

4. Cook in batches 6 to 8 minutes or until golden brown. Drizzle with chocolate syrup. Serve immediately.

SUGAR-AND-SPICE TWISTS

2 tablespoons granulated sugar

½ teaspoon ground cinnamon

1 package (about 11 ounces) refrigerated breadstick dough (12 breadsticks)

1. Combine sugar and cinnamon in shallow dish or plate. Separate breadsticks; roll each piece into 12-inch rope. Roll ropes in sugar-cinnamon mixture to coat. Twist each rope into pretzel shape.

2. Preheat air fryer to 370°F. Line basket with parchment paper; spray with nonstick cooking spray.

3. Cook in batches 8 to 10 minutes or until lightly browned. Remove to wire rack to cool 5 minutes. Serve warm.

HINT: Use colored sugar sprinkles in place of the granulated sugar in this recipe for a fun "twist" of color perfect for holidays, birthdays or simple everyday celebrations.

GRILLED CHEESE KABOBS

MAKES 12 SERVINGS

8 thick slices whole wheat bread

3 thick slices sharp Cheddar cheese

3 thick slices Monterey Jack or Colby Jack cheese

2 tablespoons butter, melted

1. Cut each slice bread into 1-inch squares. Cut each slice cheese into 1-inch squares. Make small sandwiches with one square of bread and one square of each type of cheese. Top with second square of bread. Brush sandwiches with butter.

2. Preheat air fryer to 370°F. Cook sandwich squares 30 seconds to 1 minute or until golden brown and cheese is slightly melted.

3. Place sandwiches on the ends of short wooden skewers, if desired, or eat as finger food.

CANDY CALZONE

1 package small chocolate, peanut and nougat candy bars, chocolate peanut butter cups or other chocolate candy bar (8 bars)

1 package (about 15 ounces) refrigerated pie crusts (2 crusts)

½ cup milk chocolate chips

1. Chop candy into ¼-inch pieces.

2. Unroll pie crusts on cutting board or clean surface. Cut out 3-inch circles with biscuit cutter. Place about 1 tablespoon chopped candy on one side of each circle; fold dough over candy to form semicircle. Crimp edges with fingers or fork to seal.

3. Preheat air fryer to 370°F. Line basket with parchment paper. Cook in batches 8 to 10 minutes or until golden brown. Remove to wire rack to cool slightly.

4. Place chocolate chips in small microwavable bowl; microwave on HIGH 1 minute. Stir; microwave in 30-second intervals, stirring until smooth. Drizzle melted chocolate over calzones; serve warm.

CRISPY RANCH CHICKEN BITES

1 pound boneless skinless chicken breasts

¾ cup ranch dressing, plus additional for serving

2 cups panko bread crumbs

1. Cut chicken into 1-inch cubes. Place ¾ cup dressing in small bowl. Spread panko in shallow dish. Dip chicken in dressing; shake off excess. Roll in panko to coat. Spray chicken with nonstick cooking spray.

2. Preheat air fryer to 370°F. Line basket with parchment paper.

3. Cook in batches 8 to 10 minutes or until golden brown and cooked through. Serve with additional ranch dressing.

MACARONI AND CHEESE BITES

MAKES ABOUT 4 SERVINGS

4 ounces uncooked elbow macaroni

1 tablespoon butter

1 tablespoon all-purpose flour

1 cup milk

½ teaspoon salt, divided

1 cup (4 ounces) shredded Cheddar cheese

½ cup (2 ounces) shredded Swiss cheese

½ cup (2 ounces) shredded smoked Gouda cheese

2 eggs

2 tablespoons water

1 cup plain dry bread crumbs

½ teaspoon Italian seasoning

Marinara sauce, heated

1. Cook macaroni in large saucepan of boiling salted water 7 minutes or until al dente. Drain and set aside.

2. Melt butter in same saucepan over medium-high heat. Whisk in flour until smooth. Cook 1 minute, whisking frequently. Whisk in milk in thin, steady stream; cook over medium-high heat about 8 minutes or until thickened. Add ¼ teaspoon salt. Gradually stir in cheeses until melted and smooth. Stir in macaroni.

3. Spray 6×3-inch baking pan* with nonstick cooking spray. Spread macaroni and cheese in prepared pan; smooth top. Cover with plastic wrap; refrigerate 4 hours or until firm and cold.

4. Turn out macaroni and cheese onto cutting board; cut into 1-inch pieces. Preheat air fryer to 370°F.

5. Whisk eggs and 2 tablespoons water in medium bowl. Combine bread crumbs, Italian seasoning and remaining ¼ teaspoon salt in shallow dish. Working with a few pieces at a time, dip macaroni and cheese pieces in egg, then toss in bread crumb mixture to coat. Place on baking sheet.

6. Cook in batches 2 to 3 minutes or until golden brown, turning once. Serve warm with marinara sauce for dipping.

Depending on the size of your air fryer, you may need to modify the size of your baking dish.

HAPPY APPLE SALSA WITH CINNAMON PITA CHIPS

2 teaspoons sugar

¼ teaspoon ground cinnamon

2 pita bread rounds, split

1 tablespoon jelly or jam

1 medium apple, diced

1 tablespoon finely diced celery

1 tablespoon finely diced carrot

1 tablespoon golden raisins

1 teaspoon lemon juice

1. Combine sugar and cinnamon in small bowl. Cut pita rounds into wedges. Spray with nonstick cooking spray; sprinkle with cinnamon-sugar.

2. Preheat air fryer to 330°F.

3. Cook 8 to 10 minutes, shaking occasionally, until lightly browned. Set aside to cool.

4. Meanwhile, place jelly in medium microwavable bowl; microwave on HIGH 10 seconds. Stir in apple, celery, carrot, raisins and lemon juice. Serve salsa with pita chips.

SANDWICH MONSTERS

1 package (about 16 ounces) refrigerated jumbo buttermilk biscuit dough (8 biscuits)

1 cup (4 ounces) shredded mozzarella cheese

⅓ cup sliced mushrooms

2 ounces pepperoni slices (about 35 slices), quartered

½ cup pizza sauce, plus additional for serving

1 egg, beaten

1. Separate biscuits; set aside one biscuit for decorations. Roll out remaining biscuits into 7-inch circles on lightly floured surface.

2. Top half of each circle evenly with cheese, mushrooms, pepperoni and ½ cup pizza sauce, leaving ½-inch border. Fold dough over filling to form semicircle; seal edges with fork. Brush tops with egg.

3. Split remaining biscuit horizontally; cut each half into eight ¼-inch strips. For each sandwich, roll two strips of dough into spirals to create eyes. Divide remaining two strips of dough into seven pieces to create noses. Arrange eyes and noses on tops of sandwiches; brush with egg.

4. Preheat air fryer to 370°F. Line basket with parchment paper or foil.

5. Cook in batches 6 to 8 minutes or until golden brown. Remove to wire rack; cool 5 minutes. Serve with additional pizza sauce.

TIP: Don't worry about leaking sauce or cheese—it will look like it's coming from the monster's mouth!

LAVASH CHIPS WITH ARTICHOKE PESTO

MAKES 6 SERVINGS (ABOUT 1½ CUPS PESTO)

- 3 pieces lavash bread
- ¼ cup plus 2 tablespoons olive oil, divided
- ¾ teaspoon kosher salt, divided
- 1 can (14 ounces) artichoke hearts, rinsed and drained
- ½ cup chopped walnuts, toasted*

- ¼ cup packed fresh basil leaves
- 1 clove garlic, minced
- 2 tablespoons lemon juice
- ¼ cup grated Parmesan cheese

To toast nuts, cook in preheated 350°F parchment-lined air fryer 3 to 4 minutes or until golden brown.

1. Preheat air fryer to 370°F. Line basket with parchment paper.

2. Brush both sides of lavash with 2 tablespoons oil. Sprinkle with ¼ teaspoon salt. Cut to fit in air fryer, if necessary. Cook in batches 8 to 10 minutes, shaking occasionally, until lavash is crisp and browned. Cool on wire rack.

3. Place artichoke hearts, walnuts, basil, garlic, lemon juice and remaining ½ teaspoon salt in food processor; pulse about 12 times until coarsely chopped. While food processor is running, slowly stream remaining ¼ cup oil until smooth. Add cheese and pulse until blended.

4. Serve lavash with pesto.

NOTE: You can also toast walnuts in preheated 350°F oven 6 to 8 minutes, if preferred.

SPICY BAKED SWEET POTATO CHIPS

MAKES 4 SERVINGS

1 teaspoon sugar

½ teaspoon smoked paprika

¼ teaspoon salt

¼ teaspoon ground red pepper

2 medium sweet potatoes, unpeeled and cut into very thin slices

2 teaspoons vegetable oil

1. Combine sugar, paprika, salt and ground red pepper in small bowl; set aside.

2. Place potatoes in large bowl. Drizzle with oil; toss to coat. Sprinkle with seasoning mix.

3. Preheat air fryer to 390°F. Cook in batches 15 to 18 minutes, shaking occasionally until chips are lightly browned and crisp. Cool completely.

POUND CAKE DIP STICKS

½ cup raspberry jam, divided

1 package (10¾ ounces) frozen pound cake

1½ cups cold whipping cream

1. Microwave ¼ cup jam on HIGH 30 seconds or until smooth. Cut pound cake into 10 (½-inch) slices. Brush one side of slices lightly with warm jam. Cut each slice lengthwise into three sticks.

2. Preheat air fryer to 390°F. Spray basket with nonstick cooking spray.

3. Cook in batches 5 to 6 minutes or until cake sticks are crisp and light golden brown. Remove to wire rack.

4. Meanwhile, beat whipping cream in large bowl with electric mixer until soft peaks form. Add remaining ¼ cup raspberry jam; beat until combined. Serve pound cake dip sticks with raspberry whipped cream.

CORN TORTILLA CHIPS

MAKES 6 DOZEN CHIPS

6 (6-inch) corn tortillas, preferably day-old

½ teaspoon salt

Salsa or guacamole (optional)

1. If tortillas are fresh, let stand, uncovered, in single layer on wire rack 1 to 2 hours to dry slightly.

2. Stack tortillas; cut tortillas into six or eight equal wedges. Spray tortillas generously with nonstick olive oil cooking spray.

3. Preheat air fryer to 370°F.

4. Cook in batches 5 to 6 minutes, shaking halfway through cooking. Sprinkle with salt. Serve with salsa or guacamole, if desired.

NOTE: Tortilla chips are served with salsa as a snack, used as the base for nachos and used as scoops for guacamole, other dips or refried beans. They are best eaten fresh, but can be stored, tightly covered, in a cool place 2 or 3 days.

ROASTED CHICKPEAS

MAKES 1 CUP

1 can (about 15 ounces) chickpeas, rinsed and drained

2 tablespoons olive oil

½ teaspoon salt

½ teaspoon black pepper

½ tablespoon chili powder

¼ teaspoon ground red pepper

1 lime, cut into wedges (optional)

1. Combine chickpeas, oil, salt and black pepper in large bowl; toss to mix well.

2. Preheat air fryer to 390°F.

3. Cook 8 to 10 minutes, shaking occasionally during cooking, until chickpeas begin to brown.

4. Sprinkle with chili powder and ground red pepper. Serve with lime wedges, if desired.

EGGPLANT NIBBLES

MAKES 4 SERVINGS

1 egg

1 tablespoon water

½ cup Italian-seasoned dry bread crumbs

1 Asian eggplant or 1 small globe eggplant

Marinara sauce (optional)

1. Beat egg and water in shallow dish. Place bread crumbs in another shallow dish.

2. Cut ends off of eggplant. Cut into sticks about 3 inches long by ½-inch wide.

3. Coat eggplant sticks in egg, then roll in bread crumbs. Spray with olive oil cooking spray.

4. Preheat air fryer to 370°F. Line basket with foil or parchment paper.

5. Cook 12 to 14 minutes, shaking occasionally during cooking, until eggplant is tender and lightly browned. Serve with marinara sauce, if desired.

ROSEMARY-SCENTED NUTS

1 tablespoon unsalted butter, melted

1 cup pecan halves

½ cup unsalted macadamia nuts

½ cup walnuts

½ teaspoon dried rosemary

¼ teaspoon salt

⅛ teaspoon red pepper flakes

1. Preheat air fryer to 330°F.

2. Combine butter, pecans, macadamia nuts and walnuts in large bowl; mix well. Add rosemary, salt and red pepper flakes; stir.

3. Cook 15 to 18 minutes, shaking several times during cooking. Cool completely. Store in airtight container.

GARLIC-HERB PARMESAN DIPPING STICKS

MAKES 12 SERVINGS

1 package (about 14 ounces) refrigerated pizza dough

¾ cup light garlic-and-herb spreadable cheese

¾ cup (3 ounces) shredded Italian cheese blend

¼ cup grated Parmesan cheese

½ teaspoon dried oregano

Warm marinara sauce and/or ranch salad dressing (optional)

1. Roll out dough on lightly floured surface to 12-inch square. Spread garlic-and-herb spreadable cheese evenly over bread. Top with Italian cheese blend, Parmesan cheese and oregano.

2. Preheat air fryer to 390°F. Line basket with parchment paper; spray with nonstick cooking spray.

3. Cut dough in half or thirds to fit into basket. Cook in batches 6 to 8 minutes or until golden brown. Let cool slightly.

4. Slice lengthwise into strips. Serve with marinara sauce or ranch for dipping, if desired.

KALE CHIPS

MAKES 6 SERVINGS

1 large bunch kale (about 1 pound)

1 tablespoon olive oil

1 teaspoon garlic powder

½ teaspoon salt

½ teaspoon black pepper

1. Wash kale and pat dry with paper towels. Remove center ribs and stems; discard. Cut leaves into 2- to 3-inch-wide pieces.

2. Combine leaves, oil, garlic powder, salt and pepper in large bowl; toss to coat.

3. Preheat air fryer to 390°F.

4. Cook in batches 3 to 4 minutes or until edges are lightly browned and leaves are crisp. Cool completely. Store in airtight container.

SUPER SALAMI TWISTS

MAKES 12 SERVINGS

1 egg

1 tablespoon milk

1 cup (about ¼ pound) finely chopped hard salami

2 tablespoons yellow cornmeal

1 teaspoon Italian seasoning

1 package (about 11 ounces) refrigerated breadstick dough (12 breadsticks)

¾ cup pasta sauce, heated

1. Beat egg and milk in shallow dish until well blended. Combine salami, cornmeal and Italian seasoning in separate shallow dish.

2. Unroll breadstick dough. Separate into 12 pieces along perforations. Roll each piece of dough in egg mixture, then in salami mixture, gently pressing salami into dough. Twist each piece of dough twice.

3. Preheat air fryer to 370°F. Line basket with parchment paper.

4. Cook in batches 8 to 10 minutes or until golden brown. Remove to wire rack; cool 5 minutes. Serve warm with pasta sauce for dipping.

SWEETS & TREATS

TOASTED POUND CAKE WITH BERRIES AND CREAM

1 frozen pound cake, thawed

2 tablespoons melted butter

1 cup fresh blackberries or blueberries

1 cup fresh raspberries or strawberries

Whipped topping, vanilla ice cream or prepared lemon curd

1. Cut pound cake into eight slices. Brush both sides of cake with butter.

2. Preheat air fryer to 370°F. Cook in batches 5 to 7 minutes, turning halfway through cooking, until cake is lightly browned.

3. Serve with fresh berries, whipped topping, ice cream or lemon curd, as desired.

HASSELBACK APPLES

2 medium apples, unpeeled
  Foil
2 tablespoons packed brown
  sugar
2 tablespoons finely
  chopped walnuts

½ teaspoon ground
  cinnamon
2 tablespoons butter, melted
½ cup vanilla ice cream
  (optional)

1. Cut apples in half vertically. Scoop out seeds. Lay flat side down; cut slits ⅛ inch apart almost all the way down. Place apples on foil; wrapping lightly up sides of apple.

2. Combine brown sugar, walnuts and cinnamon in small dish. Brush butter over tops of apples, letting drip inside slits. Sprinkle apples with brown sugar mixture.

3. Preheat air fryer to 350°F. Place foil-wrapped apples in basket. Cook 12 to 15 minutes or until apples are softened and browned.

4. Serve with ice cream, if desired.

NOTE: If apples brown too quickly on top, brush with additional melted butter.

CHOCOLATE-COFFEE NAPOLEONS

1 tablespoon instant coffee granules

¼ cup warm water

1 package (4-serving size) chocolate instant pudding and pie filling mix

1¾ cups whole milk plus 1 teaspoon whole milk, divided

1 sheet frozen puff pastry (half of a 17¼-ounce package), thawed

3 tablespoons powdered sugar

2 tablespoons bittersweet or semisweet chocolate chips

1. Dissolve coffee in water in small bowl; set aside to cool.

2. Combine pudding mix, 1¾ cups milk and coffee in medium bowl; mix according to package directions. Cover and refrigerate until needed.

3. Preheat air fryer to 370°F. Unfold pastry sheet; cut into three strips along fold marks. Cut each strip crosswise into thirds, forming nine squares total. Cook in batches 8 to 10 minutes or until puffed and golden brown. Remove to wire rack to cool completely.

4. Blend powdered sugar and remaining 1 teaspoon milk in small bowl until smooth. Cut each pastry square in half crosswise with serrated knife to form 18 pieces total. Spread powdered sugar icing over tops of six pastry pieces.

5. Place chocolate chips in small resealable food storage bag. Microwave on MEDIUM (50%) 30 seconds or until melted. Cut small piece off one corner of bag; drizzle over iced pastry pieces. Place in refrigerator while assembling napoleons.

6. Spoon about 2 tablespoons pudding mixture over each of six pastry pieces; layer with remaining six pastry pieces and pudding mixture. Top with iced pastry pieces. Refrigerate until ready to serve.

MIXED BERRY DESSERT LAVASH WITH HONEYED MASCARPONE

MAKES 4 SERVINGS

1½ cups assorted mixed fresh berries

2 tablespoons honey, divided

½ teaspoon vanilla

1 piece lavash bread, 7½×9½ inches

1 tablespoon melted butter

4 ounces (½ cup) mascarpone cheese

1 tablespoon julienned fresh mint leaves

1. Place berries in medium bowl; stir in 1 tablespoon honey and vanilla. Refrigerate until ready to use.

2. Brush both sides of lavash with butter; cut into four even pieces.

3. Preheat air fryer to 370°F. Line basket with parchment paper. Cook 6 to 8 minutes, turning half way through cooking, until lavash is golden and crisp. Cool 5 minutes on wire rack.

4. Stir mascarpone and remaining 1 tablespoon honey in small bowl. Spread over each piece of lavash. Top with sweetened berries. Sprinkle with mint to serve.

CINNAMON-SUGAR TWISTS

1 **package (8 ounces) refrigerated crescent roll dough**

½ **cup coarse sugar**
1 **teaspoon ground cinnamon**

1. Unroll dough on work surface. Cut crosswise into 1-inch strips. Roll strips to form thin ropes; fold in half and twist halves together. Combine sugar and cinnamon in shallow dish.

2. Preheat air fryer to 370°F. Line basket with parchment paper; spray with nonstick cooking spray.

3. Cook in batches 6 to 8 minutes or until golden brown. Spray with cooking spray; roll in cinnamon-sugar mixture to coat. Serve warm.

DOUGHNUT HOLE FONDUE

1 package (about 6 ounces) refrigerated biscuit dough (5 biscuits)

3 tablespoons butter, divided

1 tablespoon sugar

¼ teaspoon ground cinnamon

¾ cup whipping cream

1 cup bittersweet or semisweet chocolate chips

½ teaspoon vanilla

Sliced fresh fruit, such as pineapple, strawberries and cantaloupe

1. Separate biscuits into five portions. Cut each in half; roll dough into balls to create 10 balls.

2. Place 2 tablespoons butter in small microwavable bowl. Microwave on HIGH 30 seconds or until melted; stir. Combine sugar and cinnamon in small dish. Dip balls in melted butter; roll in cinnamon-sugar mixture.

3. Preheat air fryer to 370°F. Spray basket with nonstick cooking spray.

4. Cook in batches 4 to 5 minutes or until golden brown.

5. Meanwhile, heat cream in small saucepan until bubbles form around edge. Remove from heat. Add chocolate; let stand 2 minutes or until softened. Add remaining 1 tablespoon butter and vanilla; whisk until smooth. Keep warm in fondue pot or transfer to serving bowl.

6. Serve with doughnut holes and fruit.

CHOCOLATE CHERRY TURNOVERS

1 package (8 ounces) refrigerated crescent roll dough

¾ cup semisweet chocolate chips, divided

½ cup canned cherry pie filling

1. Unroll dough onto clean work surface; separate into four rectangles. Press perforations firmly to seal. Cut off corners of rectangles with sharp paring knife to form oval shapes.

2. Place 1 tablespoon chocolate chips on half of each oval; top with 2 tablespoons pie filling. Sprinkle with additional 1 tablespoon chocolate chips. Fold dough over filling; press edges to seal. Crimp edges with fork, if desired.

3. Preheat air fryer to 370°F. Spray basket with nonstick cooking spray.

4. Cook in batches 8 to 10 minutes or until golden brown. Cool on wire rack 5 minutes. Melt remaining chocolate chips and drizzle over turnovers. Serve warm.

FRIED PINEAPPLE WITH TOASTED COCONUT

1 large pineapple, cored and cut into chunks

½ cup packed brown sugar

1 teaspoon ground cinnamon

½ teaspoon ground nutmeg

½ cup toasted coconut*

Ice cream or whipped cream (optional)

Chopped macadamia nuts (optional)

Maraschino cherries (optional)

To toast the coconut in the air fryer, place coconut in small ramekin. Cook in preheated air fryer at 350°F for 2 to 3 minutes or until lightly browned.

1. Place pineapple chunks in large bowl. Combine brown sugar, cinnamon and nutmeg in small bowl; sprinkle over pineapple. Toss well. Refrigerate 30 minutes.

2. Preheat air fryer to 370°F. Spray basket with nonstick cooking spray.

3. Cook 6 to 8 minutes or until pineapple is browned and lightly crispy. Sprinkle with coconut. Serve with ice cream or macadamia nuts, if desired. Garnish with maraschino cherry.

APPLE PIE POCKETS

- 2 pieces lavash bread, each cut into 4 rectangles
- 2 tablespoons melted butter
- ¾ cup apple pie filling
- 1 egg, lightly beaten with 1 teaspoon water
- ½ cup powdered sugar
- ⅛ teaspoon ground cinnamon
- 2½ teaspoons milk

1. Brush one side of each piece of lavash with butter. Place half of the pieces, buttered-side down, on work surface. Spoon 3 tablespoons pie filling in center of each lavash, leaving ½-inch border uncovered. Using pastry brush, brush border with egg wash. Top with remaining lavash pieces, buttered-side up. Using tines of fork, press edges together to seal. Use paring knife to cut three small slits in center of each pie pocket.

2. Preheat air fryer to 370°F. Line basket with parchment paper.

3. Cook in batches 8 to 10 minutes or until crust is golden and crisp. Remove to wire rack; cool 15 minutes.

4. Combine powdered sugar, cinnamon and milk in small bowl; whisk until smooth. Drizzle over pockets; let stand 15 minutes to allow glaze to slightly set.

APPLE-CRANBERRY TURNOVERS

1 sheet frozen puff pastry (half of a 17¼-ounce package), thawed

FILLING

1 large Granny Smith apple (about 7 ounces), peeled and diced (about 1 cup)

2 tablespoons dried cranberries

2 tablespoons packed dark brown sugar

1 tablespoon butter

¼ teaspoon ground cinnamon

⅛ teaspoon ground allspice

TOPPING

1½ teaspoons granulated sugar

⅛ teaspoon ground cinnamon

1 tablespoon butter, melted

1. Unfold puff pastry.

2. Place filling ingredients in medium saucepan. Cook and stir 2 to 3 minutes over medium heat until apples start to soften. Remove from heat; cool completely.

3. Cut pastry into four squares. Brush edges with water. Spoon ¼ cup of the apple mixture in center of each square and fold to create a triangle. Seal edges by pinching seams with fork. Place on baking sheet. Cover and refrigerate 30 minutes.

4. Preheat air fryer to 370°F. Remove turnovers from refrigerator. Make small cut on top of each turnover. Cook in batches 8 to 10 minutes or until puffed and golden brown.

5. For topping, combine granulated sugar and cinnamon in small bowl. Brush equal amounts of butter on each warm turnover; sprinkle with cinnamon-sugar mixture. Serve warm or at room temperature.

AIR-FRIED S'MORES

2 whole graham crackers, broken in half

Foil

2 marshmallows

1 package (1.5 ounces) milk chocolate candy bar, broken in half

1. Place two graham cracker squares on two sheets of foil. Top each with marshmallows. Gather foil around graham crackers.

2. Preheat air fryer to 370°F. Cook 1½ to 2 minutes or until marshmallows are browned.

3. Remove carefully from basket. Top marshmallows with chocolate bar halves and remaining graham cracker squares. Bring sides together to create sandwich.

INDEX

METRIC CONVERSION CHART

VOLUME MEASUREMENTS (dry)

1/8 teaspoon = 0.5 mL
1/4 teaspoon = 1 mL
1/2 teaspoon = 2 mL
3/4 teaspoon = 4 mL
1 teaspoon = 5 mL
1 tablespoon = 15 mL
2 tablespoons = 30 mL
1/4 cup = 60 mL
1/3 cup = 75 mL
1/2 cup = 125 mL
2/3 cup = 150 mL
3/4 cup = 175 mL
1 cup = 250 mL
2 cups = 1 pint = 500 mL
3 cups = 750 mL
4 cups = 1 quart = 1 L

VOLUME MEASUREMENTS (fluid)

1 fluid ounce (2 tablespoons) = 30 mL
4 fluid ounces (1/2 cup) = 125 mL
8 fluid ounces (1 cup) = 250 mL
12 fluid ounces (1 1/2 cups) = 375 mL
16 fluid ounces (2 cups) = 500 mL

WEIGHTS (mass)

1/2 ounce = 15 g
1 ounce = 30 g
3 ounces = 90 g
4 ounces = 120 g
8 ounces = 225 g
10 ounces = 285 g
12 ounces = 360 g
16 ounces = 1 pound = 450 g

DIMENSIONS

1/16 inch = 2 mm
1/8 inch = 3 mm
1/4 inch = 6 mm
1/2 inch = 1.5 cm
3/4 inch = 2 cm
1 inch = 2.5 cm

OVEN TEMPERATURES

250°F = 120°C
275°F = 140°C
300°F = 150°C
325°F = 160°C
350°F = 180°C
375°F = 190°C
400°F = 200°C
425°F = 220°C
450°F = 230°C

BAKING PAN SIZES

Utensil	Size in Inches/Quarts	Metric Volume	Size in Centimeters
Baking or Cake Pan (square or rectangular)	8×8×2	2 L	20×20×5
	9×9×2	2.5 L	23×23×5
	12×8×2	3 L	30×20×5
	13×9×2	3.5 L	33×23×5
Loaf Pan	8×4×3	1.5 L	20×10×7
	9×5×3	2 L	23×13×7
Round Layer Cake Pan	8×1½	1.2 L	20×4
	9×1½	1.5 L	23×4
Pie Plate	8×1¼	750 mL	20×3
	9×1¼	1 L	23×3
Baking Dish or Casserole	1 quart	1 L	—
	1½ quart	1.5 L	—
	2 quart	2 L	—